Re:
Quin

Selected Other Works by Robert Buckeye

Covering Ground

Pressure Drop

Setting a Table

The Munch Case

Still Lives

Re:
Quin

Robert
Buckeye

DALKEY ARCHIVE PRESS
CHAMPAIGN / LONDON / DUBLIN

First edition, 2013

Buckeye, Robert.

Re: Quin / Robert Buckeye. – First edition.

pages cm

Includes bibliographical references.

ISBN 978-1-56478-887-0 (pbk. : alk. paper)

1. Quin, Ann, 1936-1973–Criticism and interpretation. I. Title.

PR6067.U5Z55 2013

823'.914–dc23

2013008513

Partially funded by a grant from the Illinois Arts Council, a state agency, and Middlebury College

www.dalkeyarchive.com

Cover: design and composition by Mikhail Iliatov

Printed on permanent/durable acid-free paper and bound in the United States of America

For Peter Anastas

Table of Contents

" . . . how each of us manages to make more evident his own resistance. For that is the way a man comes to core. By way of, the discovery of, his own resistance."

—Charles Olson

INTRODUCTION

"There was no beginning . . . We'd stopped living. The beginning did not, would not, exist prior to the end . . . Hallucinations within the hallucinations that was already speech. The body of a dead princess as a metaphor for literature."

–Stewart Home

IN THE FALL of 1964, I heard Malcolm X speak at Wayne State University in Detroit. Several months before Congress passed the Tonkin Gulf Resolution and in Philadelphia, Mississippi, Andrew Goodman, Michael Schwerner and James Chaney had been murdered. The murder of John Fitzgerald Kennedy the year before had set off something, a premonition that was chilling, as if we had awakened to a world we did not believe, but no one, except perhaps Malcolm, anticipated what was to follow. Malcolm himself gunned down. Viola Liuzzo, a Detroit housewife, murdered by the Klu Klux Klan in Selma, Alabama. Martin Luther King shot. Robert Kennedy picked off. Riots in the cities, including Detroit three years later.

Malcolm was electric. Had there been anyone as charismatic, as challenging? Anyone whose mind as sharp as a knife? I still do not think so. Democracy had been a lie, Malcolm said, matter-of-factly, as if, of course, we all knew that, equality a myth, freedom for those with "nothing left to lose." If we did not do something.

Malcolm paused, and the question hung in the air.

Well.

There was a storm coming.

§

What followed is by now an old story. For others, a story they don't want to hear. One that does not go away. Assassinations and turmoil *worldwide. Protests* against racial, gender and class inequality. Outrage against the Vietnam War ("Vietnam, Vietnam, Vietnam," Michael Herr writes, "we've all been there.") Rioting in Watts, Detroit, Newark, Chicago. Student protests in Warsaw, Mexico City, Paris, Berlin, across America after Kent State. Bloody Sunday in Derry, the Prague Spring, Solidarity, Che Guevara shot in Bolivia, Israel's Six-Day War, a military takeover in Greece, Rudi Dutschke shot in Berlin. Its quasars were, J. G. Ballard was to tell us in *Love & Napalm:Export U.S.A.*, "Malcolm X, beautiful as the trembling hands in tabes dorsalis; Claude Eatherly, migrant angel of the Pre-Third; Lee Harvey Oswald, rider of the scorpion."

Things could not go on as they had before. "The entire world was on the verge of radical transformation," Eliot Weinberger writes in *Written Reaction*, "from the structure of society and state to the details of body ornament." The Stones and bellbottoms. Free love and free spirits. Equality as never before, possibility unthought of. Resistance and revolution. In the streets of Paris in May, 1968, French students took for their cry a Situationist International slogan, "Under the Paving Stones, the Beach," to emphasize the need to discard the old ways of doing business to find a way to live that was free, fulfilling, just.

Some writers felt that their writing had not only to reflect the times, but also, in some way, lead them. The business of literature could not be conducted as it had been before. These writers dismissed traditional methods and ignored mainstream venues for new ways in which to write and alternative sites in which to situate their writing—bars were not uncommon. Little mags far from New York, London or Paris proliferated. "If it was poetry that brought the unsettled debts of history back into play," Greil Marcus writes in *Lipstick Traces*, "the unsettled debts of history brought forth poetry." What they wrote, Weinberger adds, appeared, "like oracles."

Ann Quin's four novels bracket the Sixties. If establishment Anglo novels continued to dominate critical attention, there were writers like Quin whose books escaped, challenged or ignored tradition. Novels by Amis, Bellow, Davies, Fowles, Graham Greene, Mary McCarthy, Murdoch, Naipaul, Philip Roth, and Updike were contested formally from one side by John Berger, Gass, Hawkes, Aidan Higgins, Paul Metcalf, Pynchon and Wurlitzer, among others, and culturally from the other side by novels that resisted the imperatives of a middle class, increasingly petit bourgeois, reading public, including Burroughs's *Naked Lunch* (1959), Trocchi's *Cain's Book* (1960), Lessings's *The Golden Notebook* (1962), Selby's *Last Exit to Brooklyn* (1964), J. J. Phillips's *Mojo Hand* (1966), Edith Templeton's *Gordon* (1966), Sorrentino's *The Sky Changes* (1966), J. G. Ballard's *The Atrocity Exhibition* (1969), Douglas Woolf's *Spring of the Lamb* (1972), any number of novels by B. S. Johnson.

For the most part these writers remain marginal, if not forgotten. Phillips disappeared. Woolf, a Harvard graduate, lived hand to mouth all his life and never drew the attention of the establishment. Trocchi withdrew into methadone treatment for drug addiction. Templeton's *Gordon* is less than a trivia question. After a reading at a college, Metcalf, who is a grandson of Herman Melville, was asked by a professor where he got his doctorate. Of course, today, a Melville would be expected to find his Harvard at Harvard, not on a whaling ship. (In fact, Metcalf attended Harvard but left.) At the end of his life, Selby ended up in the classroom, where he joined Sorrentino and others in the great rush of the academy to find creative writers for its students who suddenly wanted to be writers.

If the times shaped Quin, she also played a part in their shaping. She is, moreover, a more radical writer than those I mentioned, most of whom retain traces of literature, however we understand them, that Quin discards or disdains. Only Burroughs, Metcalf and Woolf challenge literature in ways that she does. It is not that they teach us how to read them in reading them, but that our reading of them forces us to question the enterprise itself. In a footnote at the end of *69 Things to Do With a Dead Princess*, Home contrasts Quin with Hemingway, Gertrude Stein and Beckett, noting, "our attention could be more usefully directed towards Ann Quin." Her writing may yet survive its defeat, but its defeat surely determines literature in our times.

§

In a 1972 interview with John Hall in *The Guardian*, Quin says that one day her mother did not feel like reading to her and suggested the seven-year-old girl go into the garden and write a story of her own. Quin writes about a princess, prince and witch, dramatizing the triangulation of a relationship she would never resolve; the girl, as the woman, who would never know whether she would be a princess or witch; whether, in fact, one was also the other.

In autumn, at the end of the fifties, at a holiday festival, she chooses to be a Catherine wheel, a firework named after the medieval torture device whose victim's limbs are threaded through the spokes of a wheel and raised on a pole for hungry vultures and crows to pick.

In the posthumously published, "Eyes That Watch Behind the Wind," she surfaces in Mexico in a picture in a market (one would guess taken by Quin from a Munch print), "A nude woman clutched by a skeleton death figure, behind her, with arms outstretched as if ready to devour her also, a masked surgeon."

§

Well, yes.

We could not know the beginning before we knew the end.

THE LIFE

"A beautiful but withdrawn woman who might have strayed from the pages of The Atrocity Exhibition*."*
–J. G. Ballard

ON MARCH 17, 1936, Ann Quin was born in Brighton, the "unreal city" of T. S. Eliot's *The Waste Land*, a seaside resort whose life revolves around both the need to escape and the one to seek. Graham Greene's *Brighton Rock* is set there and Aubrey Beardsley grew up there. For those raised in Brighton, as Quin was in petit bourgeois circumstances, the carnival of summer did little to compensate for desolate, barren winter months. Winter only emphasized Brighton was not a life and one had to escape it, which the carnivalesque celebration of summer sanctioned by suggesting other possibilities of living, if not a glimpse of something like utopia. If Quin had to escape difficult circumstances time and time again in her life, not always of her own making, she never ceased to seek a life better than the one she had.

After she was born, her father, Nicholas Montague, a failed opera singer, abandoned them, and her mother was forced to raise Quin alone. She often beat her daughter and sent her off to the Convent of the Blessed Sacrament to live and study. The convent was, Quin was to say later in "Leaving School," a brief memoir, "A ritualistic culture that gave me a conscience.

A death wish and a sense of sin. Also a great lust to find out, experience what really was." In the convent, she was fascinated by the color of nuns' bloomers and imagined what was behind Christ's loincloth. Books from the public library—notably Dostoyevsky's *Crime and Punishment* and Woolf's *The Waves*, but also Chekhov, Lawrence, and Hardy—helped her escape from everyday life, if they did not also accelerate her withdrawal into dream and fantasy. "I created dreams out of everyday situations until nothing ever seemed what it appeared to be," she notes.

At fourteen she met her half brother for the first time and fell in love with him. When he died five years later, Quin writes, "I saw myself as Antigone." As it turned out, her life followed that of Antigone more than she might have thought. She was never at home anywhere and thought of herself as banished. To seek forbidden love was characteristic of her need to stand outside. Death was always near.

At seventeen, she joined a theater company as an assistant manager and, after six weeks, auditioned for the Royal Academy of Dramatic Arts, but failed. "I expected a stage," she writes of her audition, "even a platform, instead a smallish room, brightly lit; ten or twelve people faced me. I began, froze, asked to start again, but was struck dumb, and rushed out, silently screaming down Gower Street." It would not be the last time she was struck dumb, and silence at crucial points would come to determine not only that she be a writer, but also what kind of writer she became, "Where what I had to express, say, would be my own interpretation, my own vision, and be accepted by an unseen audience."

Despite her failure to make a career on stage, she drew upon theater not only in her fiction but also in her life. When her brother disappeared, she saw herself as Antigone. She played

Caliban in school. In *Berg*, Berg's father is a vaudeville performer, and the book itself is modeled loosely after Hamlet. Tramps living under piers in Brighton serve as a Greek chorus in *Berg*. In *Three*, the principals stage a masque in an empty swimming pool, and its protagonist, S., had wanted to be Bernadette in a play in school. *Passages* is littered with references to Greek mythology, much of it made into drama.

§

In order to support herself, Quin attended secretarial school and became proficient in typing and shorthand, and the succession of menial jobs she took to make ends meet in London, Brighton and Cornwall followed her all her life. As a typist at Hutchinson's, she got a sense of the world of publishing, while living the artist's life in a dark garret in Soho. She completed a novel, *A Slice of the Moon*, which did not get published. "Days spent in sleepwalking," she comments. "Through Abstract[s] of Titles; letters that never varied. But the world of love waited me every evening. I lived for that, would have gladly died for it."

Working in a hotel in Cornwall, she suffered a breakdown. "Being a waitress was not unlike going on the stage," she writes. "I had little time for writing . . . I collapsed one morning . . . I lay in bed for days, weeks, unable to face the sun. If I went out into the garden, I dug holes and lay in them weeping. I woke up in the middle of the night screaming, convinced my tears were rivers of blood." She saw a psychiatrist, and decided, "The loneliness of going over the edge was worse than the absurdity of coping with day to day living."

She worked at St. Dunstan's home for the blind, lived with her mother, and read Sartre's *Being and Nothingness*. She moved to Paris, became a nanny with a French family, once again took shorthand and typing tests, hoping to land a job with NATO, but did not succeed. She returned to Mevagissey, a Cornish fishing village where she soon became head waitress and enjoyed gardening, swimming and fishing in the off season, but as guests arrive for the summer, staff criticized her work and she fled.

§

She completed a second novel, *Oscar*, which also did not get published and left for Greece and Italy in what would become an increasingly common pattern of escape. On her return, she asked a friend how one of the teenage lovers she met in Italy would adapt if she brought him to England and added, "I'm having ghastly nightmares about [the] novel [*Berg*] and meeting publishers who look at my legs and not my manuscript," (Kitchen, 57).

In 1964, her first novel, *Berg*, was published. "Here was a working-class voice from England," Giles Gordon writes in his introduction to the novel, "quite unlike any other, which had absorbed the theatrical influences of John Osborne and employed the technical advances of the nouveau roman."

She met Robert Creeley, who was in England on a reading tour, and had an affair with him. "She can be, variously, the expected demure young lady, or else the barstool swinging drunken broad," Creeley writes of the woman who is surely Quin in *Mabel: A Story*. "It doesn't really seem to matter that much to her. She is an age hard to determine. Very young, quite probably, five or six, in her own mind, but also markedly old, looking down on it, whatever, some other persons or circumstances, from that abstract wiseness."

He arranged that she receive the D. H. Lawrence Fellowship in New Mexico, the first woman to receive the fellowship. She also received the Harkness Fellowship for the most promising Commonwealth writer under the age of 30. In America, she experimented increasingly with drugs (LSD and peyote), stayed on the road (New York, Mexico, the Bahamas, the Berkeley Poetry Conference), and sought out sex wherever she was.

§

The frenzy that drove her on her arrival to America dissipated at moments and she saw America as a possibly idyllic place she might live in, far from the dank, dreary England that depressed her. She thought of the day Creeley drove her to the D. H. Lawrence ranch in May, "trees blooming, birds warbling, the mesa stretching out immensely against the backdrop of the mountains" (Faas, 303). She writes Nigel Jones about her apartment in San Francisco: "Have found a simply lovely apartment, in a crazy yellow old house on a barge, right on the water, a large wooden paneled room, with windows overlooking Bay and hills in the distance, where I know I will be basically much happier, and will be able to settle down to some real writing, which up to now has been more or less nil—what with all my wanderings and so on" (Jones, 65).

In "Ghostworm," a posthumously published story, the female protagonist lies on a mesa in New Mexico with her lover and watches rain in the distance, thinking how different it is from rain in England, "So much time spent in a country where hearing it meant just another day of bloody weather. And voices commenting cold today yes but not as cold as yesterday looks like rain. Could I return to that?"

§

Three was published on her return to England in 1966, underlining in its title the triangulation in all her novels. In *Berg*, a son searching for his father becomes involved with the woman who is with his father. In *Three*, a husband becomes involved with their roomer, S., whose wife is also drawn to her. In *Passages*, a woman searches for her lost brother with her lover. In *Tripticks*, a man follows and is followed by his ex-wife and her lover. "The most naturally and delicately gifted novelist of her generation," one review says of *Three*. "The writing is at once generous, lyrical, and spare," another notes.

Quin took a job as secretary in the painting school of the Royal College of the Arts and began work on *Passages*. In a life increasingly undone by crises, her work on this novel, which takes four versions, is the most damaging. After she sent the novel to her publisher, she contracted glandular tuberculosis. While she convalesced, she revised its galleys, "dreaming in fact of months, years maybe, of being in a sanatorium somewhere in the mountains and writing masterpieces. Instead I had to face the world again, and the problems of being published." She went to Ireland and Greece, as part of her recovery but also, once again, to escape.

When *Passages* was published in 1969, the most personal of her works and the one she considers most important, Quin won an Arts Council grant. "The dream had been realized," Quin writes, "but reading what I had written seemed someone else's dream. A kind of involuntary commitment. And like Camus I became aware that, 'There is in me an anarchy, a frightful disorder. Creating costs me a thousand deaths, for it involves an order and my whole being rebels against order. But without it I could die scattered'" ("Leaving School," 68). In the last half century, there are few novels as good as *Passages* that have been as much, as unjustly, neglected. "Ultimately unlike any other work," Brian Evenson and Johanna Howard wrote in the *Review of Contemporary Fiction* (66).

Quin spent the Arts Council grant on drugs, clothes, and a three-month odyssey to Ireland, Denmark, Norway, and Sweden, where police discovered her one day rolling naked in a snowdrift. Her publisher, Marion Boyars, brought her back to London. "If it hadn't been for a few guardians," she writes a friend, "I might well have been in the Cassel or some such place undergoing various 'shock' treatments to 'rehabilitate' me back into this insane society." She underwent electro-shock treatment in Sweden and again on her return to London. ("Psychotherapeutic talk that beats around the bush, electroshocks, and chemical preparations," Jean Amery notes in *At the Mind's Limits*, "are ready to make someone who was different in one's own way into someone different in quite another way.") She lost her job at the Royal College of the Arts and spent time at a religious retreat.

§

When she returned, she worked as a waitress in Notting Hill. In her depression, she slept 14 hours one day and spent a numbing Christmas holiday with her mother. "Ate, slept & watched tele most of the time—wot a life?" To what extent repeated electroshock therapy affected her cannot be precisely determined, but its impact on her writing is clear. *Tripticks* (1972), the novel that follows her electroshock treatment, is different from her earlier works and not nearly as powerful. Illustrated by a lover, Carol Annand, it is a savage assault on an America obsessed by commerce, advertising and media, a road novel from hell, written as if it is the frenzy of one last gasp.

Afterwards, in the by now familiar repetition compulsion that bleeds from her life into her fiction, she traveled to Switzerland and once again suffered a breakdown, unable to speak for some time, and spent a month in a hospital in London. She went on social security and moved to a smaller flat in London. She sublet the flat she had left and when the tenant failed to pay the bills, real estate agents cleaned it out, dumping everything into the garbage, including two novels by Quin.

§

In the summer of 1973, Quin applied to the University of East Anglia, so that she might work with Malcolm Bradbury, although registrars questioned her competence for college. Before she could enter East Anglia, her father, whom she sought out, died; her mother had an accident and Quin returned to Brighton to take care of her; her latest lover left. In August, she walked into the ocean, like Virginia Woolf, whose novel, *Waves*, Quin read in childhood to escape her oppressive life.

§

In autumn at the end of the fifties, Quin and two friends, Paddy Kitchen and Tim Rendle, named themselves after fireworks at a holiday festival. Rendle is the rocket, Kitchen the Roman candle, and Quin the Catherine wheel, named after the medieval torture device whose victim's limbs are threaded through the spokes of a wheel and raised on a pole for hungry vultures and crows to pick. It was all, always, her body she put at risk.

SEARCH

"As her schizophrenia deepened she embarked on a series of impulsive journeys all over Europe, analogues perhaps of some mysterious movement of her mind."

-J. G. Ballard

THE WRITING OF travel is always a tale of escape, adventure and the exotic with the underlying but unspoken possibility of sexual freedom. Gauguin in Tahiti is the model; Byron in Greece; Margaret Fuller in Italy. It is a story in which its protagonist escapes his life at home and gains a freedom he does not, ordinarily, have. "Isn't traveling a purification," Walter Benjamin notes, "the overcoming of settled passions that are attached to one's accustomed environment, and hence an opportunity to develop new ones?" (*Selected Writings II*, 645). Away from home, after all, the traveler is anonymous. He may seek out an untouched and exotic distant land, in part, because the simpler lives of its people are seen to be more authentic than his own. ("For moderns," Dean MacCannell writes in *The Tourist*, "reality and authenticity are thought to be elsewhere in other historical periods and other cultures, in purer, simpler life styles."

At the same time, the traveler is at risk in one way or another. The ways in which he understands and controls his life at home may not work here. He may not know the language where he is.

What is strange may never become familiar. He may be preyed upon as much as he preys. In the literature of travel, hardship and danger are always possible; uncertainty at some point a certainty; ignorance a given. Whether it is metaphorical or not, nature threatens, and fear lingers at the edge of consciousness of the stranger in a strange land. He might lose his way at any point and experience that dizzying moment in which he does not know where he is or what might happen.

These circumstances play out differently for women. If the woman traveler finds she has greater independence on the road, she is also more vulnerable, since she leaves behind the regulated circumstances of home. If the male traveler may prey sexually upon the native—he may do away from home what he might not do at home—the female traveler may be both predator and prey—the native may assert a power over the female traveler his encounters with the male traveler deny him. If the travel narrative, then, is about desire, escape and freedom, it is also about capitalism, first world domination, sexual politics.

As much as the traveler puts home behind him, he does not escape it. In Italo Calvino's *Invisible Cities*, Marco Polo, who has traveled the length and breadth of the Great Khan's Chinese dynasty, is asked by the Khan to describe the cities he has seen, because the Khan has seen only a part of his empire. At one point the Khan asks why Polo never describes his own city of Venice. "Every time I describe a city," Polo answers, "I am saying something about Venice."

In *A Seventh Man*, John Berger discusses how guest workers bring with them reminders of home in their luggage—a photograph, locket, figurine or scarf—which they do not need in the country where they work, but which are essential to keep the memory of home alive in a foreign land. No matter how far from home we may be, there are reasons why it remains with us.

If travel is a threshold the traveler seeks, it may also be a boundary. He may be limited or bound by life away from home as much as he is by his own circumstances. On the road, he lacks the security the familiar life provides, even if his uncertainty and resulting anxiety may force him to discover things about himself he does not know. "For what gives value to travel is fear," Albert Camus writes in *Lyrical and Critical Essays*. "It breaks down a kind of inner structure we have. One can no longer cheat—hide behind the hours spent at the office or at the plant (those hours we protest so loudly, which protect us so well from the pain of being alone)."

There is also travel that is involuntary, that of the exile, criminal, political emigre or nomad, those dispossessed in one way or another, who are driven by circumstances beyond their control to go from one place to another, never to arrive at a place they can call their own. In *At the Mind's Limits*, Jean Amery notes that "One must have a home not to need it." In her discussion of her early years in Algeria, Hélène Cixous explains why Algeria—"My Algeriance" she calls it—determined the writer she became. She was born in a Jewish family in Germany and moved to French Algeria as a girl. In Algeria, she was no longer German, and as a Jew, she was an Arab to the French. To the Arabs (who she felt affinities with), she was French. "I felt perfectly at home, nowhere," Cixous concludes in *Stigmata*, which caused "a certain writing [to be] engendered that does not settle in, it does not inhabit its house, it escapes, it goes off without turning back."

§

If Quin's fiction mirrors her own incessant, unending travel, it also, as Calvino and Berger argue, never leaves Brighton (or England) and is, if not more so, a journey, as Ballard suggests, that she follows in her mind. The dream world the girl imagines to escape the world around her becomes for the woman (and novelist) the means to seek a better life and escape the one she finds oppressive. "Life," T.J. Clark agues, "must become the game desire plays with itself" ("The Revolution of Modern Art and the Modern Art of Revolution," 3). It is the game Quin plays.

Increasingly, however, Quin's search becomes desperate, at times little more than drift, aimless, at times despondent, a kind of searching her protagonists are driven towards as if it is involuntary. They do what they cannot not do. "I feel like a leaf blown down, drifting," Quin writes in a letter to Paddy Kitchen. "There seems nothing to catch on to, and any moment I will be swept and lie rotting in the gutter" (Kitchen, 53).

Her novels play out the possibilities of a search she herself follows: a son for the father who left (*Berg*); a couple for S., their roomer, who has disappeared (*Three*); a woman for her dead brother (*Passages*); a man for his ex-wife (*Tripticks*—the title itself suggests the itinerary of travel). In fact, the ostensible search hides the real one for the self they do not have, the one they flee from, do not understand. That this search is more internal than external only complicates its resolution, if it does not make it impossible.

At what point does the external search (ever) realize the internal one? How does one trace the geography of desire, particularly, "if madness is another trip,—like death"? (*Passages*, 67) In Quin's world, fantasy, dream, memory, imagination, perception and experience are, as R. D. Laing argues in *The Politics of Experience*, "simply different modalities of experience, none more 'inner' or 'outer' than any other." Increasingly her characters find they can realize their internal search only through an external one elsewhere. In Quin's world, search is synonymous with travel.

§

Though it is set in the Brighton of Graham Greene's *Brighton Rock*, *Berg* lacks the specificity of the Greene novel. Greene uses actual names and locations of hotels, landmarks, and seafront amusements in Brighton. In contrast, Quin's description is surreal, always interior, associative, fragmentary if not random, more poetry than prose, nearly claustrophobic. "Quin's imaginary," Stewart Home calls it (169).

In *Berg*, everything is filtered through the mind of Berg and we are never certain whether it comes from the inside or the outside, whether it is something he says or thinks. Quin moves from what Berg is thinking to what someone else says without drawing a distinction between them. Letters quoted from Berg's mother may be no more than imagined conversations in his head. He describes women on a Brighton dance floor as "plants, tall, thin, short, fat rubbery plants as though released suddenly from their pots" (68). Narrative disappears into stream of consciousness and surfaces as if it is somehow no longer narrative, discursive maybe, drifting certainly, obsessive always.

It is, Quin feels, too conventional of a novel, though she was to follow its methods and develop them with greater risk in later novels. It has too much of an intricate plot for the writing that, she understands later, she must do. Berg tracks his father to Brighton and follows him in order to kill him, because of his abandonment of the family and the disgrace he has given his mother, even if Berg himself has left home to escape his mother. In killing his father, he will not only avenge his mother's disgrace and escape the meaninglessness of his life but also replace his father in his mother's life. In a series of inadvertent, comic mistakes, Berg kills his father's ventriloquist dummy instead of his father and replaces his father with his mistress. The man who occupies the room Berg rented before moving in with his father's mistress seems suspiciously like his father.

"[*Berg*] is a Graham Greene thriller as if reworked by a somewhat romantic Burroughs," Giles Gordon writes in his introduction to *Berg*, but it is too much of a noir thriller for Quin. "*Berg* was a necessary struggle to free myself from inhibiting constrictions," she notes. Like Cixous, but for different reasons, Quin must find a method that comes from her life, as Cixous does for hers, and to do that she cannot follow the usual conventions of fiction. "The only book that is worth writing," Cixous writes in *Three Steps on the Ladder of Writing*, "is the one we don't have the courage or strength to write." It is to be the book after *Berg*. Again and again.

If travel for her protagonists never leaves Brighton behind, it is, nevertheless, a place they must leave. Brighton can be no more than, "the survival of those who preferred remaining halfway," Berg thinks, "never accepting, or rejecting, aware only of the urge to defeat boredom, [their] little perversions never slapped across the front page." England is a place, Quin notes in "Ghostworm," "where I can no longer belong."

They fear they will be dragged down by the tawdriness, ugliness and mediocrity around them, because they see it in themselves, despite their dreams and ambitions. It is not so much that the everyday kills, but that they will not be able to rise above it. Berg remembers his experience at village dances, "reclining in a corner, terrified of so much sophistication, everyone that much more adult, more knowledgeable in the rules of the social game."

In Quin's fiction, there are always reasons to go, even if the search is one her characters follow in their minds and can have no destination or end. A search for the lost father. That for the lost brother. A woman who may have committed suicide. The adventure of travel and the exotic. A lover. The possibility of a lover.

"As long as she has a catalogue of places," the unnamed female protagonist of *Passages* says of her search for her lost brother, "a file of photographs, addresses. Men who resemble, if only by a gesture, a hand raised, a large ring on the middle finger." If it is not one thing, it can be another. Her characters find reasons to justify the search they make, even if at moments they despair of ever succeeding. "Days like this are taken up with nostalgia," the woman's lover in *Passages* thinks, "longing for some other climate, another person, another love, until they are all spread out like a vast geographical map. There are so many routes."

The foreign land is never what it promises to be, and is as much an alien world, if not more so, than the one at home. In New York, the aversion of one of her protagonists to what she sees—"what looked like bundles of old clothing, which moved when she passed, and she saw white bony hands clasp a bottle, another a syringe"—is complicated not only by her alienation —"Confronted by her own strangeness"—but also by her recognition that away from home she is at risk in ways she is not at home. In Quin's fiction, the lives of natives are never more authentic than that of the traveler, only more oppressive.

If travel enables her characters to escape the limits of class in England, class nevertheless makes them uncomfortable as tourists, the outward and visible sign of first world dominance. In "Ghostworm," the female protagonist feels, "helplessness in the face of [the natives's] defeat, their resigned acceptance of life conquered by death." At moments, she thinks she would like to be as they are, "part of the room, chairs, table." In *Passages*, where the couple searches for the woman's lost brother on a Greek island, the man thinks of the town they are in as, "a city where every street declares its defeat." Impotence, in one form or another, is always at issue.

Difficulty only drives the search more intensely. "Don't get bogged down," the woman's lover in *Passages* thinks, "risk all, what is there, but the risking? So. She risks with her body, her imagination (her heart/mind?)." In their need for greater intensity—to go beyond at all costs, not to escape but to realize a sense of themselves—her protagonists seek out sex, whenever or wherever possible. "No sense of who touched her," one thinks, "who she was stripped by, who woke her as soon as she tried to sleep."

Their frenetic efforts to live life more fully bring only an emptiness that is less disturbing than traumatic—"boredom at the level of panic, a yawn that comes out a scream," the ex-husband of *Tripticks* thinks. Insanity threatens, and death. "I see only the emptiness," the unnamed female protagonist in *Passages* thinks. "I look in all the corners and don't find myself." It is the ground zero all her protagonists reach.

If desire drives one, there is nothing to do but continue, since search predicated upon desire cannot be realized (when the impossible, Julia Kristeva notes in *Powers of Horror*, "constitutes its very being"). ("Another climate needed," the woman of *Passages* thinks. "Another place. No sense of place here. Perhaps not even other places. But a place . . . So let us begin another journey. Change the setting. Everything is changing, the country, the climate. There is no compromise now. No country we can return to. She still has her obsession to follow through and her fantasies to live out."

§

Though the search in Quin's fiction mirrors ones in her life (that for the father, the brother) or places she has been (America, Mexico, Greek islands), her writing is less about travel than it is about finitude, and in that it distinguishes itself from much travel writing. There is no place away from home she can be herself. Life on the road is no more satisfying than it is at home, even if—yes—it offers possibilities, particularly sexual ones, she cannot realize at home. Travel has been less a threshold for new possibilities than a recognition that nothing has changed.

As much as travel has been her own decision, it was also a decision she could not help but make. Like the exile, she must leave. Like the political emigre, her ideas force her from home (the game desire plays with itself always threatens the status quo). Like the nomad, she must follow the shifting sands. There can never be arrival. She is prepared to lose her way, because she has already lost it, and must lose what keeps her lost to find her way, even if she fears it may not be possible. As we must lose our way, too, in reading her. As much as her writing may reflect the conventions of travel writing, it follows rules of its own making.

One story her writing tells is that it cannot be told as literature as we understand it. Or it refuses to do so. We may read in her notes, fragments and marginalia an incompleteness which underlines a skepticism about what literature can do. She must twist or turn art; push through or beyond it; destroy it if necessary. How can it be otherwise? That her travel is determined by "some mysterious movement in her mind," as Ballard puts it in *The Atrocity Exhibition*, demands that her writing be nothing less. "Desire is not form," Gilles Deleuze and Felix Guattari argue in *Kafka: Toward a Minor Literature*, "but a procedure, a process."

For Quin, there is, I feel, a second consideration for her refusal of tradition. That has to do with the relation of her writing to the place literature occupies in society. To make of her story merely literature. To understand how it will be read in a middle class society, what purposes it will serve. Quin distrusts it, despairs of it, at every moment threatens to abandon what she cannot let go. Nevertheless, she must write, because writing is her means of resistance against a world which holds a gun to her head. Her writing is deeply subversive, a rupture of middle-class pieties. The serious artists are enemies of art, George Oppen reminds us (Oppen, 8).

Sex

"I did fantasize a lot about being in bed with a man and a woman, and I introduced a boy friend of mine to a girl friend of mine and they both knew it was one of my fantasies, so we explored it together. It was important to my writing that it extended the fantasy . . . this actual experience was so far beyond the fantasy that I found it very, well, you could say enlarging . . . [In America] I went into it very easily, and again it was very beautiful. Very much like a dance . . . you don't know whose hand it is, or whose mouth, and this is extraordinarily exciting."

–Ann Quin

QUIN DRAMATIZES HER sexual fantasies, obsessions and experience in her fiction. The brother she loves appears in other brothers: in *Three*, S. writes in her journal, "What happened to John? Scholarship to the University. At the age of sixteen. Ran away. Never heard of again." In "Ghostworm," the married American lover asks the English woman he is having an affair with, "Were you looking for Christ then? Ah God no. A father? No—a brother." In *Mabel: A Story*, Robert Creeley writes of a woman based on his relationship with Quin: "She wants the man, so to speak, to fantasize their relation, be the bleeding moors boy, be the brother." Most dramatically in *Passages*, the female protagonist searches for her missing brother with her lover.

Her fantasy of an affair with her father is an obsession of

S. in *Three*. She remembers him practicing high Cs before concerts; the time he gave her a Japanese fan and had her sit on his lap; the times he whipped her; the weekends she visited him, "Where I enlarged on the conspiracy of not being his daughter, perhaps his mistress."

Her fiction, moreover, is a catalog of sexual practices: threesomes (*Three*, *Passages*, *Tripticks*, "Ghostworm"); violence, often whipping (*Three*, *Passages*, *Tripticks*, "Ghostworm"); cross-dressing (*Three*, *Berg*); gender reversal (*Three*); sex with strangers (*Three*, *Passages*, "Ghostworm"); masturbation (*Berg*, *Three*); oral sex (*Passages*, *Three*, *Tripticks*, "The Unmapped Country").

In *Tripticks*, the narrator says of his second wife that, "Her first lover apparently left her his private flat designed for orgies, complete with floor mirrors and elaborate camera setup for making movies of all the fun. Copy of Kraft-Ebbing in hand she went through all the paces, developing a real yen for the Aristotelian perversion." Her four novels come out of a Sixties sensibility, however, and Quin did not have to go to Kraft-Ebbing to embrace the sexual freedom the Sixties promised.

§

If we are to understand how sex drives the search for life and self, we need to backtrack to Quin's childhood in Brighton, the whippings her mother gave her, the lust for transgression the convent school taught her, an attraction for what was absent and forbidden (the missing brother and father), her withdrawal into dreams and fantasies to escape the world of her childhood. ("The monotony keeps the fantasies moving," the female protagonist of "Ghostworm" thinks.)

For the woman and writer, sex was not only a means to escape the oppressive life of England but also one to find herself, even if she could not escape the prison house of desire. It was further an attack, if only implicitly, against a relentlessly repressive bourgeois society. Quin linked a better society to sexual fulfillment. The pursuit of pleasure for its own sake would be the first step to free us from an inherently repressive bourgeois society.

Her assault on bourgeois goodness is based, in part, on its denial of intimacy. "A deformation of good," Theodor Adorno characterizes it in *Minima Moralia*. (Although there may be a tendency to conflate Quin's life with that of her characters, we must remember that the protagonists of *Berg* and *Tripticks* are men.) If sex is a source of knowledge, a path to discovery, the possibility of utopia, it is also, R. D. Laing writes, as much ontological security as it is a means of gratification or escape.

We go furthest with our bodies, her fiction reads, and it is at those moments we discover who we are. If her mother's whippings result in a predilection for whipping by some of her characters, we need to understand that their need to feel, however extreme the solution, needs to be seen in context of a society that controls the individual at every point and in so doing deadens feeling, if not kills it. Body knowledge instructs in a way no other teaching does. "Wanting to take in his history while taking him in her mouth," the female protagonist of "Ghostworm" thinks.

This means that her characters must let go of themselves, even if their letting go can be threatening, dangerous, if not destructive. "There is no fullness of pleasure," Benjamin notes in *The Arcades Project*, "unless the precipice is near." Violation, if not violence, is always latent. Nevertheless, her characters seek the possibility of possibility in sex, the intensity beyond which one cannot but go, a life like no other. "We were invisible," S. thinks of a lover she spends a night with in a hotel. "Contained in our bodies, that had crossed borders never before realized."

§

All her novels involve triangles: in *Berg*, the son finds his father with a woman and becomes involved with her as well; in *Three*, a couple tries to discover why S., their roomer, has disappeared, presumably a suicide; in *Passages*, a woman searches for her missing brother with her lover; in *Tripticks*, a man follows and is followed by his ex-wife and her lover. Threesomes are the subject, if not subtext, of her posthumous fiction.

If triangular relations offer possibilities couples do not have, they are also more dramatically unstable and uncertain than what is for the couple in itself not always stable, certain or clear. In any relationship, sex is always an, "Expression of a dance that takes its own course" (*Three*, 72). We follow where it takes us, whatever it might be, and, at any moment, may face the unknown. By the time Quin writes *Tripticks*, however, its dance has become little more than the frenetic hedonism of those who want to escape the meaninglessness and absurdity of an America driven by consumption, pleasure, self-righteousness and piety.

The goal of the threesome, however it is understood, is to complete the triangle. As much as sex may be seen as a means to regain a paradise lost, one cannot be innocent, except, willfully, to blind oneself. Sex always connects itself to other triangles—family, social, religious, bureaucratic and economic—that determine its values. In this sense, Quin's emphasis on sex is political in its argument for a better life in conscious opposition to the one that exists. She does nothing less than put family, religion, and society in the dock.

In *Three*, S., the female protagonist, writes in her journal, "Possessed. Be possessed. To possess." All sex, as this conjugation implies, is triangular in which anything inside or outside oneself or the other, anything they do, may, at any moment change—shift, dissolve or enlarge—become an assemblage of its own making. "A world could be as small as the navel," S. thinks. Fantasy may bring reality into its orbit or reality drag fantasy along to, "Gain another level, an added dimension, preferably bringing them both with me," S. thinks, so that something new, neither one nor the other, results.

§

Three is dedicated to "Bobbie and Bob," the American couple Quin was sexually involved with, and the novel is closely linked not only to them but also to other elements in Quin's life. S., who is a roomer in the home of Ruth and Leonard, writes in her journal of her missing brother who ran away from home, of the oppressive school she had gone to, her fantasy of being her father's mistress. As the relationship between S., Ruth and Leonard develops it foreshadows a threesome that is not realized before S. disappears.

S. has recently had an abortion and rents a room from Ruth and Leonard, "to begin to begin again." She sees how miserable and frustrated they are—like their hamster which claws constantly at its cage—and how they have become the target for local hoods. During a mime play S. has talked Ruth and Leonard into performing in their empty swimming pool, locals shower them with clods of earth. Earlier, they broke the windows of the greenhouse where Leonard keeps orchids.

They don masks and white robes for the mime play and the narrative, as S. conceives it, is how, "two reject one, or one rejects two, or all three reject each other, or equally accept." As their relationship develops, it mirrors the mime play, which, as S. describes it, describes the circumstances of a threesome. Leonard has an affair with S. Ruth is drawn to S. and masturbates wearing S.'s clothing. When Leonard is away on a trip, Ruth invites S. into her room to drink whiskey and asks S. to brush her hair. Ruth rejects Leonard and has rejected him for years. Leonard rapes Ruth and when she is asleep watches a home movie of a naked girl at the ocean (likely S.) and is overwhelmed with emotion. S. complains in her journal of a man (likely Leonard) who cares only for his own orgasm, indifferent to hers.

The mime play is a carnivalesque staging, in which those who perform in it may assume roles of their own choosing. For the moment they may escape the roles they have chosen in society or those which have been assigned them. When Leonard thinks back to the Second World War when he was in solitary confinement, he notes that even there he had a part to play. In the home movie he watches, the naked woman is wearing a mask, as if even naked she plays a role. He mentions to Ruth that S. liked to swim naked and asks why she never does that. Ruth answers that S. is "a bit of an exhibitionist," suggesting it is a role she projects.

S. understands that the roles we play serve society as much as they do ourselves, if not more so; that we live our lives less than we perform them. In her journal, S. recalls how she was treated by doctors and psychiatrists during her pregnancy, "knowing as much as I did that whatever I said didn't really matter . . . They seemed to gain almost a perverse satisfaction from enquiring how many men I had in fact slept with in the past year." She comes to realize that Ruth and Leonard see her much as the medical profession does and begins to exploit their attraction to her in order to bring them down, "Pursued by a compulsion, to jeopardize such a bourgeois stronghold."

She neither succeeds in her effort to challenge their relentless petit bourgeois lives nor change her own. (Although it is clear after S.'s disappearance that Ruth and Leonard have been strongly influenced by her, it is doubtful they will do anything to change their lives.) "The possibility of what might have been slides away," S. writes in her journal, "to what is left." She disappears, presumably a suicide, having left a note that, "nothing will change." All that we know for certain is that her boat capsized and a note is found in her coat, which was recovered.

§

The story is told after S.'s disappearance. Ruth and Leonard read S.'s journals and listen to tapes she has made to understand why, if possible, she has disappeared. They look over their own journals and read one another's. Leonard looks at the home movie he has made, presumably, of S. They talk to one another. Why has S. disappeared? What was it about her that drew them to her? Just who exactly was she? They do not succeed. S.'s journals are written as free verse, and are elliptical at best. They only raise questions, which make S. more mysterious than ever. Ruth and Leonard's journals are closely guarded. At one point, S. comes across little black crosses in Leonard's journal, "which seem to be some kind of code," and she is afraid they have to do with her, but she knows Leonard will never acknowledge their relationship, as he will acknowledge little else. "No country we can return to," are the last words S. writes in her journal before her disappearance. We must answer her accusation as best we can, if we can. The best art demands no less.

Their interest is hardly disinterest. Both Ruth and Leonard have used her, and are complicit in S.'s death. Like those in the medical profession who terminate her pregnancy or, in fact, those in society in general. They place S. in their world, refuse to see hers, and insist she must live as they do. In *Three*, Quin turns the lamp away from S. and onto those who question her. We must keep this image of their apparent disinterest masking a deeper prurient interest in mind in order to place Quin's fiction in relation to a middle-class reading public. The uses made of literature are not cheering.

SILENCE

"I opened my mouth, but no words. Only the words of others I saw, like ads, texts, psalms, from those who had attempted to persuade me into their systems. A power I did not want to possess."

—Ann Quin

AT HER AUDITION for the Royal Academy of Arts, Quin was struck dumb. Alan Burns reports that at a reading at the ICA in London Quin, "did her Quin thing, that is to say she came onto the stage and she just sat and looked at people, she wouldn't say a goddam word! She just stared, she either implied or she actually stated that we sort of 'think-communicate,' we can communicate more in silence than with someone actually putting the words across" (Coe, 405). After the publication of *Tripticks*, Quin suffered a breakdown in Switzerland and was unable to speak for some time.

For Quin, writing has to speak against the dominant, relentlessly petit bourgeois voice, however she can manage it. Against that which silences (and which did silence her at various points in her life). There are no signs for her to follow, however at times she may convince herself there are. Nothing to guide her. No progress. The impossibility of writing. The impossibility of not writing. "Writing like a dog digging a hole, a rat digging its burrow," Deleuze and Guattari write of Kafka (18). "And to do that, finding his own point of underdevelopment, his own patois, his own third world, his own desert."

To learn, Quin had to unlearn. She had to break down, disrupt, dissolve. Writing becomes interruption, rupture, dissociation. Although Quin may retain narrative, increasingly it becomes vestigial, as if it were an afterthought. The ostensible search in her fiction is less passage than obsession, less progress than movement, however that can be characterized. Her novels are nonlinear, elliptical, associative: a coherence of fragments (marginalia, journals, illustrations) alongside interrupted and uncompleted narrative, sketchy character, uneven tone.

Her language is often as spare as a Beckett stage. "Day after day, the nights slid across, rolled under. Windows closed." Or it is dashed off, the worst cliches, careless, as if she does not quite believe what she writes. Or it is notes, that would be fleshed out, ordinarily, later in a text. "Travesty?/a little. Now./Then." The effect is often dizzying, disorientating, vertigo.

She introduces free-verse poetry (*Three*); notes and lists (*Passages*, *Tripticks*); illustrations, catalogs, interviews and correspondence (*Tripticks*). *Three* brackets alternating, often conflicting, narratives told in part in journal entries and tape-recordings. Her writing is complicated further, if not disrupted, by the disappearance of punctuation, the absence of inverted commas to characterize dialogue, abrupt shifts from first person to third, the completion of a sentence at the beginning of the next paragraph. The interpretative, controlling voice of the author is more often than not absent. Her description is often that of a camera. In *Tripticks*, she employs William S. Burroughs's cut-up method, splicing into the text passages from *Time* and *Life* magazines, among others.

After *Berg* and *Three*, Quin stops naming characters, although in *Three* her protagonist is simply S. In *Passages*, neither the lovers nor the missing brother (who is John in *Three*) are named and in *Tripticks*, an ex-husband chases and is chased by ex-wives. To name is to define, to place. To be without name is to be no one from nowhere. Her unnamed characters, however, are not meant to be everyman, merely those who don't know who they are. The search Quin's characters follow—that mysterious movement of mind Ballard refers to—cannot be limited, confined as it were, by naming, since their search is as uncertain as their identity.

At times, her writing may seem to be nothing more than stream-of-consciousness (which she makes an effort to distance herself from after *Berg*), particularly in her practice to elide the distinction between something inside someone's mind and that outside it. There is a repetition compulsion at work in her writing, forcing her beyond. (Freud argues that the compulsion to repeat is fundamental to the death instinct.) Its effect may be similar to that of stream-of-consciousness in its associations linked by the trajectory a mind follows. That her writing may be the surreal, disorienting, often claustrophobic activity of the mind at work, however, does not mean that we can limit it to a psychological reading.

Quin's achievement is that she never learned how writing should be written. In her interview with John Hall in *The Guardian*, she comments that she does not choose a subject or form for a book. "If the emotion is there," she continues, "the energy takes over, and the form and content follow." In *Tripticks*, the ex-husband thinks that, "The experience existed only within its own context on its own terms. A certain rhythm. A nervous montage. Trips not on established trails." A way of writing that is a dream of writing. "There are often narratives, but very seldom writing," Marguerite Duras says in *Writing*.

§

Passages is told in alternating accounts of an unnamed woman who seeks her long lost brother on Greek islands and that of her lover who accompanies her. The search for the lost brother mirrors the one they undertake for themselves. The woman's story is narrative; his a journal. Several episodes recur in their differing accounts. Notes on the margin of his journals are annotations he makes, but other margin notes on Greek mythology may or may not have been taken down by him.

"I opened the shutters," the woman writes at the beginning of the novel. "Town huddled above the sea. Thin shadows of cypresses. She stood over him, he pushed her down onto her knees. I drew the curtains." Quin shifts from first to third person and back to draw our attention to the women the woman is—the I who stands aside observing what the she does, as if she were someone else, not the I, or perhaps one of the shes the I might be. At times the I must see herself not as I, but as a third person, someone perhaps not her, someone she does not want to be, someone she might want to be. Why she must do so explains, in part, why she must seek her missing brother. To find the brother she loves is to be made whole again.

That Quin uses 'she' to describe what seems to be the beginning of sexual activity or at least some sort of submission tells us that in this instance it is the she who sees herself as another, who may want or choose to be treated as an other as she engages in sex. If Quin uses sex in her fiction as a means of discovery, the possibility of a life beyond the one she has, it may also be no more than an effort to control the other or submit to him.

The I who draws the curtains may be the I who has returned

to herself after sex. It may be the I whose action is a figurative gesture—drawing the curtains—to distance herself from her recent sexual activity. It may be an action that takes place at a time separate from the one that forced her to her knees. Disruption of time in her writing is common, mirroring the turmoil in her characters. For protagonists who obsessively follow a search they do not understand, who seek out sex to take them beyond their everyday life, time can never be more than malleable. Her use of the continuous present ("Hands pulled blinds up, down") further emphasizes that the past is as much today as tomorrow will be. All moments repeat themselves and cannot be escaped.

Much of the woman's journal has the effect of montage in film. "We sat at the bar," begins one scene. "Avoided looking in the mirror opposite. He glanced occasionally sideways. A circle of wetness on polished wood she made many circles from. Swift turns his head made." Here, Quin follows a cliche camera cut, that, say, of a body on the floor, a gun in a hand and a horrified expression on a face. The reader must connect the dots himself—write the story—as the moviegoer does, since the writer has not intervened to explain, direct or emphasize. ("The montage explodes the novel," Benjamin notes, "blows it up structurally, but also stylistically" [*Selected Writings II*, 301].) The absence of the controlling voice of the author changes what the story is.

§

If the lover's journal comments about their search not only for the missing brother but also for themselves, it also gives his interpretation of her actions that her account does not give us. "She risks with her body," he writes, "sketches her dreams on his skin, makes love out of the day's rhythms." He understands further that her effort to follow where her body takes her has to do, in part, with her effort to return to the imagined paradise of her fourteenth year when she found her brother and was in love with him. "She wants to recapture her youth," he comments, "not accepting she has lost hers. She makes love with men younger than herself (the age her brother disappeared)."

That she sees fantasy to be real ("She has her own lucidity in fantasies," he notes) and madness merely another experience ("She likes to think people look upon her as essentially quite mad") complicates his efforts to understand her. He realizes that he too must risk madness to be with her. "Almost a prerequisite for any lover she has . . . as if madness is just another trip." At the same time, it is what draws him to her. Her desire for madness gives his its own license.

When she tells him, "I feel as though I'm on loan from the underworld," he wonders what role he should play. "Does she expect me to play Orpheus? The bleeding head singing always." The ways in which he tries to understand himself are even less successful. "What does waking up in this shuttered room mean," he thinks. "Sounds of the city—all is foreign. What am I doing here, what is the point of this laughter, these gestures, this woman whose legs I part?"

§

In his discussion of El Lissitzky, T. J. Clark argues in *Farewell to an Idea* that we cannot speak of his art without understanding in whose name El Lissitzky speaks. How we write defines who reads us. What we say determines how we are seen. Those who use metaphor, simile and symbol will not understand Quin. If this is, first of all, a question about technique, it is not only a question about it. Quin's writing stands outside because she stands outside. We cannot understand her writing from inside the castle.

"The survival of artworks," Benjamin notes, "should be represented from the standpoint of their struggle for existence" (*Selected Writings III*, 141). That for the most part Quin's books are no longer in print and her writing known to few only magnifies the struggle she had to undergo to get them not only written but also published. For Quin, publication was no compensation for the life stacked up inside. "Modernism's disdain for the world and wish for a truly gratuitous gesture in the face of it," Clark writes, "are more than just attitudes: they are the true (that is, agonized) form of its so-called purism. Wilde and Nietzsche are this agony's spokesmen, Rimbaud's its exemplary life" (*Farewell to an Idea*, 8). Quin puts herself in their company. Once, she says. Give silence its silence back.

Death

"[Suicide] is no longer the crime of a dark and gloomy temperament, . . . but an answer to the oppressive provocations of existence, especially the passage of time, in the stream of which we are swimming along and watching ourselves drown."

—Ann Quin

It is no accident that death beckoned. The long twentieth century is a chronicle of those who chose to leave it. In "Everyone Knows Somebody Who's Dead," B. S. Johnson (in one of his last essays before his own suicide) wonders why so many people he had known had ended their lives, "dying before what I had imagined to be their times, simply jacking it all in, for one reason or another," including Quin whose courage he admired. She refused to "live by illusion." For some it was the only answer possible to a world which increasingly denied existence at every turn. "Modernity must stand under the sign of suicide," Benjamin notes, "an act which seals a heroic will that makes no concessions to a mentality inimical toward this will" (*Selected Writings IV*, 45).

For Quin the signs were everywhere. Education in the convent seen to be a death wish. The disappearance of her brother. Her absent father and his death shortly after she meets him. Love, always love, but no love. Breakdown after breakdown. The loss of two novels. Electroshock treatment. Naked in a snowdrift in Sweden. Fed intravenously in Stockholm and once again given ECT. Unable to speak. Hospitalized. Unable to speak. Hospitalized. Her friend, Paddy Kitchen, notes that she found phrases in letters Quin wrote to her, "which, in retrospect, made me understand that the prospect of death was always present in her life."

Quin writes of suicide directly only once in her fiction (Berg thinks of it briefly only to dismiss it). In *Three*, S. disappears, leaving an apparent suicide note, presumably having drowned, as Quin was to do later. That death is an undeniable presence in her fiction, however, is inescapable. Death of one kind or another is the fear, desire or obsession which drives the search her characters follow, that triggers their desire. Aly Berg has come to kill his father, but has run away from his own life ("the futility of everything," he thinks, "especially the game of human relationships"); the woman's brother in *Passages* is likely already dead.

If we are to have a sense of the pervasiveness of death in her fiction, we need once again to return to her childhood. Quin was petite bourgeoisie, and if we understand class to be a consideration in her need to escape, we also cannot ignore it in her fear of failure. "Class is a name," Clark writes in *The Painting of Modern Life*, "for that complex and determinate place we are given in the social body; it is the name for everything which signifies that a certain history lives us, lends us our individuality." If the petite bourgeoisie aspires to be middle class, he also fears falling back among those below him. At the same time, Quin feared her need to be free would force her to be with those who had been cast out by society. Why that fear manifested itself in a sense of death is the argument I wish to make.

§

At the end of *Berg*, Berg is asked by his father's mistress, who he has moved in with, "Aly love what are you staring at?" She has asked him to peel potatoes, tells him they should get new curtains in the apartment, that she has got a new cat. At this moment he sees the domestic life of the petite bourgeoisie he fears. A life which is death. "The survival of those who preferred remaining halfway, never accepting, or rejecting, aware only of the urge to defeat boredom, [their] little perversions never slapped across the front page." Berg is helpless in the face of a life he cannot escape.

Quin writes *Berg* to escape her history. It is why all her books get written. Why the search her characters follow, of necessity, takes them away from Brighton to America, Mexico and Greek islands, even if these places are as alien as the Brighton they left, and into increasingly desperate sexual activity as a means to transcend if not escape themselves. Place changes nothing (in fact, away from England, her characters realize the inequities of class, gender and race more clearly). Sex provides only a momentary release, which must be sought again and again.

If it is the petite bourgeoisie they must escape, it is the Other they fear, who they may become if they fail. In *Berg*, Berg is threatened by tramps under piers by the water in Brighton. In *Three*, Leonard is attacked by local hoods who destroy his greenhouse and then throw clods of dirt over them while they perform a mime in their drained swimming pool. In *Passages*, the female protagonist is oppressed by the poverty of the natives she sees on Greek islands. At the end of *Tripticks*, the ex-husband finds himself helpless, his fate to be determined by native Americans at an Indian reservation in New Mexico.

In the posthumous story, "Eyes That Watch Behind the Wind," the female protagonist is made uncomfortable in Mexico by natives. Drunks spit at her, beggars clutch at her, boys throw stones and shout out "*Gringa.*" She does not want to think about how they live, "confronted by huddled shanties in front of middle-class apartment boxes." Their "helplessness in the face of their death, their resigned acceptance of life conquered by death" oppresses her. She cannot accept the death they see to be part of life, because she sees their life to be a living death.

At some point, her characters must face the death in life they fear, whether that be the life of a petit bourgeois or that of an outcast, but their responses shift from book to book. Berg sees himself unable to escape his life. After her abortion, S. becomes a roomer at Ruth and Leonard's home hoping for a new beginning until she realizes that "nothing will change" and disappears, presumably a suicide. In the search for the brother in *Passages*, the lovers search for a life better than the one they have, even if they understand that it might not be possible. Though the search for the missing brother becomes increasingly an excuse for their failure to find better lives, they do not relinquish it. At the end of *Tripticks*, the ex-husband faces what is certainly his own death after a nightmare odyssey across America.

§

If *Tripticks* is a conventional road novel in which its protagonist, the ex-husband, pursues and is pursued by his three ex-wives across America, there is no search, goal or freedom to his odyssey, only flight and a savage assault on an America of unbridled consumerism, greed, pieties and unchecked individuality.

Quin sees sex, particularly perverse sex, to be the constant fixation of an obsessively religious people. ("I stripped bananas and thrust them up her," the ex-husband says, "half way, ate the rest, poured sour cream over her and buried my tongue, fingers in the remaining pink areas . . . Basically these games were an attempt to make sure something exciting happened every day.")

Cliches are the American *lingua franca*. ("Beautiful as Aphrodite," the ex-husband describes his first ex-wife, "wise as Athena, swifter than Mercury, stronger than Hercules." Of himself, he says, "he could hurdle skyscrapers, leap an eighth of a mile, raise tremendous weights, run faster than a streamline train.")

Banality passes for wisdom. ("I had the uneasy feeling," the ex-husband thinks at a conference, "that people talked to themselves, in a language devised for each other, . . . at conferences held for each other, supported by agencies formed for each other. And all done in the self-important atmosphere of addressing themselves to the problems of the world, which is their responsibility to find solutions for.")

America a land where dreams change as rapidly as channels. ("If you come filled with dreams, it may happen that your dream changes about every 15 minutes.")

"It is not that the petty bourgeoisie in America *has* power," Clark writes, "but that its voice has become in the years after 1945, the only one in which power can be spoken" (*Farewell to an Idea*, 388). Although Quin uses Burroughs's cut-up method in *Tripticks*, includes lists and catalogs, extensive quotation from advertising and the media, adds illustrations, for the first time she uses the voice of the petite bourgeoisie to speak through. The tone of the book is agitated, rage if not mania, as if Quin knows she cannot write this way. The text is littered with Post-it notes, as if she needs to remind herself why she writes.

§

"Independence of expression has now become almost unthinkable." (31)

"My greatest accomplishment while I remain here may be my mere survival." (37)

"When fantasy has the weight of fact; and fact the metaphorical potential of fantasy. The experience existed only within its own context, on its own terms." (64)

"My one and only defence soon became silence." (67)

"I just want to be noticed not attacked." (165)

§

At the end of his cross country flight, the ex-husband has picked up a hitch-hiking Indian and is taken by him to a reservation in a remote part of New Mexico where he realizes he is to be judged by the Indians and likely condemned (with his first ex-wife and her lover in the crowd). He climbs onto one of the roofs of their buildings to escape, uncertain what to do, while black, shrouded figures of what seem to be an Inquisition follow him.

"I discovered a breathing space," he thinks before they reach him, "a space before the scream inside me was working itself loose." The scream can be a pulpit, he thinks, "an extension of my voice, my skin, my dreams." But there is no pulpit, no possibility, no escape. "I opened my mouth," he says, "but no words. Only the words of others I saw, like ads, texts, psalms, from those who had attempted to persuade me into their systems. A power I did not want to possess. The Inquisition."

§

In *The Unmapped Country*, an unfinished novel published posthumously, Quin provides not only a summation of her work but also an acknowledgment of its defeat. "Once there had been the subterranean language with the underground forces," she writes. "If speech at all then it was the spaces between words, and the echoes the words left, or what might be really meant under the surface."

§

Hall begins his interview, "Reassuring preface specially for Mrs. Quin of Brighton: please don't be alarmed by quotes attributed to your daughter Mrs. Q. She is alive and well and living off social security and Calder and Boyars (yes, there is a difference.) In any case," he concludes his aside to Quin's mother, "these are only words, and can't hurt you" (Hall, 8). One cannot imagine a more nasty, patronizing and dismissive interview. The scream that has been Quin's pulpit, an extension of her voice, skin and dreams, has been silenced by those who control, establish order, oppress. By those she resists.

Any writer has but a single story to tell, Cesare Pavese argues in *This Business of Living*, one, "which moves him most fiercely and to which he always turns" (173). Again and again, Quin returns to the search for a life beyond the one she has, to the silence which can be her only answer to the world. If her first three novels end by not ending (at the end of *Three*, S. promises a note), then *Tripticks* is an end game. For Quin, there never could be arrival. Every road led to the same place. "Art, in our culture," Clark argues, "finds itself more and more at the limits, on the verge of emptiness and silence" (*Farewell to an Idea*, 407).

Works Cited

Adorno, Theodor. *Minima Moralia*. London: New Left Books, 1951. Translated by E. F. N. Jephcott.

Amery, Jean. *At the Mind's Limits*. Bloomington, IN: Indiana University Press, 1980. Translated by Sidney Rosenfeld and Stella P. Rosenfeld.

——. *On Suicide; a Discourse on Voluntary Death*. Bloomington, IN: Indiana University Press, 1999. Translated by John D. Barlow.

Ballard, J. G. *The Atrocity Exhibition*. San Francisco: Re/Search Publications, 1990. [In an annotation, Ballard comments about Ann Quin.]

——. *Love and Napalm: Export U. S. A.* New York: Grove Press, 1969. [Claude Eatherly was the pilot who flew the lead plane over Hiroshima and gave the go-ahead signal to drop the first atomic bomb.]

Benjamin, Walter. *The Arcades Project*. Cambridge, MA: Harvard University, 1999. Translated by Howard Eiland and Kevin McLaughlin.

——. *Selected Writings Volume 2: 1927–1934*. Cambridge, MA: Harvard University, 1999. Translated by Rodney Livingstone and others.

——. *Selected Writings. Volume 3: 1935–1938*. Cambridge, MA: Harvard University, 2002. Translated by Edmund Jephcott, Howard Eiland and others.

——. *Selected Writings. Volume 4: 1938–1940*. Cambridge, MA: Harvard University, 2003. Translated by Edmund Jephcott and others.

Berger, John. *A Seventh Man*. New York: Viking Press, 1975.

Buckeye, Robert. "Some Notes on Ann Quin," *House Organ* 18(Spring 1997). 12–13.

Burns, Alan. Quoted in Coe.

Calvino, Italo. *Invisible Cities*. New York: Harcourt Brace Jovanovich Inc., 1972. Translated by William Weaver.

Camus, Albert. *Lyrical and Critical Essays*. New York: Vintage books, 1970.

Cixous, Hélène. *Stigmata; Escaping Texts*. London and New York: Routledge, 1998. Translated by Keith Cohen and others.

——. *Three Steps on the Ladder of Writing*. New York: Columbia University Press, 1993.

Clark, T. J. *Farewell to an Idea*. New Haven and London: Yale Universitiy Press, 1999.

——. *The Painting of Modern Life*. New York: Alfred A. Knopf, 1985.

Coe, Jonathan. *Like a Fiery Elephant: The Story of B. S. Johnson*. New York: Continuum, 2005.

Creeley, Robert. *Mabel: A Story*. London: Marion Boyars, 1976.

Deleuze, Gilles and Felix Guattari. *Kafka: Toward a Minor Literature*. Minneapolis: University of Minnesota Press, 1986. Translated by Dana Polan.

Duras, Marguerite. *Writing*. New York: Lumen Books, 1998. Translated by Mark Polizotti.

Evenson, Brian. "Introduction." *Three*. Normal, IL: Dalkey Archive Press, 2001. vii–xiii.

Evenson, Brian and Joanna Howard. "Ann Quin." *The Review of Contemporary Fiction* XXIII:2 (Summer, 2003). 50–75.

Faas, Ekbert. *Robert Creeley: A Biography*. Hanover and London: University Press of New England, 2001. 302–312.

Fox, Christine. "Ann Quin (1936–1973) Lyrics from the Lacuna." Internet citation. 4/17/2005. 7 p. http://www.pavilion.co.uk/star/AQ.html.

Gordon, Giles. "*Berg*, an introduction." *Berg*. Normal, IL: Dalkey Archive Press, 2001. vii–xiv.

Hall, John. "Landscape with Three-Cornered Dances." *The Guardian* (29 April, 1972). 8. Portrait.

Herr, Michael. *Dispatches*. New York: Alfred A. Knopf, 1977.

Home, Stewart. *69 Things to do with a Dead Princess*. Edinburgh: Canongate, 2002. [Home's complete comment on Quin reads: "Avoiding Ernest Hemingway, I detour instead towards Ann Quin. Disliking Hemingway, I detour towards Ann Quin. Avoiding Stein, I detour instead towards Ann Quin. Disliking Stein, I detour instead towards Ann Quin. Feeling Beckett is too obvious a point of reference, I detour instead towards Ann Quin. Despite ongoing rumours of a B. S. Johnson revival, I feel our attention could be more usefully directed towards Ann Quin."]

Jacobi, Mary. "Home's Stead." *Village Voice* (February 19–25, 2003). 59.

Johnson, B. S. Quoted in Coe.

Jones, Nigel. "Too Far Out." *The Printer's Devil* (Summer 1966). 60–69.

Kitchen, Paddy. "Catherine Wheel: Recollections of Ann Quin." *London Magazine* 19:3 (June 1979). 50–57. Portrait.

Kristeva, Julia. *Powers of Horror; An Essay on Abjection*. New York: Columbia University Press, 1982. Translated by Leon S. Roudiez.

Laing, R. D. *The Politics of Experience*. New York: Pantheon Books, 1967.

"Lovers." Review of *Passages*. Times Literary Supplement (April 3 1969). 341.

MacCannell, Dean. *The Tourist: A New Theory of the Leisure Class*. New York: Schocken Books, 1976.

Mackrell, Judith. "Ann Quin" in *Dictionary of Literary Biography* Vol. 14. Detroit: Gale Research, 1983. 608–614.

Marcus, Greil. *Lipstick Traces: A Secret History of the Twentieth Century*. Cambridge, MA: Harvard University Press, 1989.

Oppen, George. "Selections from George Oppen's *Daybook*," *The Iowa Review*, 18:3 (Fall 1988), 1-9.

Papke, Mary E. "What do Women Want?" *Context* No. 11 (2002). 12–13.

Pavese, Cesare. *This Business of Living: Diaries 1935–1950*. London: Peter Owen Limited, 1951. Translated by A. E. Murch.

Quin, Ann. *Berg*. London: John Calder, 1964.

——. "Every Cripple Has His Own Way of Walking." *Nova* (Dec. 1966). 127–135.

——. "Eyes That Watch Behind the Wind." *Signature 20: A Signature Anthology*. London: Calder & Boyars, 1975. 131–149.

——. "Ghostworm." *Tak Tak Tak* Number 6 (1993). 61–89.

——. "Leaving School - XI." *London Magazine* (July 1966). 63–68.

——. "Motherlogue." *Transatlantic Review* 32 (1969). 101–05.

——. "Never Trust a Man Who Bathes with his Fingernails." *El Corno Emplumado* 27 (July 1968). 8–16.

——. *Passages*. London: Calder and Boyars, 1969.

——. *Three*. London: Calder and Boyars, 1966.

——. *Tripticks*. London: Calder & Boyars, 1972. Illustrated by Carol Annand.

——. "From 'The Unmapped Country'; An Unfinished Novel." *Beyond the Words: Eleven Writers in Search of a New Fiction*. London: Hutchinson, 1975. 255–74. Edited by Giles Gordon.

——. [Review of Passages]. *London Magazine* 9:3 (June 1969). 100–01.

The Revolution of Modern Art and the Modern Art of Revolution. English Section of the SI. 6/12/01. 1-12. http://www.notbored.org/english.html

Stevick, Philip. "Voices in the Head: Style and Consciousness in the Fiction of Ann Quin." *Breaking the Sequence: Women's Experimental Fiction.* Princeton: Princeton University Press, 1989. Edited by Ellen G. Friedman and Miriam Fuchs. 231–239.

Sward, Robert. "Poets at Novels." *Poetry* 112:5 (August 1968). 353–356.

Weinberger, Eliot. *Written Reaction.* New York: Marsilio Publishers, 1996.

Wheeler, Kathleen. "Reading Kathy Acker." *Context* 9 (2001), 5–6.

Willmott, R. D. A *Bibliography of Works by and about Ann Quin* London: Ealing College, 1981.

ROBERT BUCKEYE is the author of several books of fiction, including *Still Lives*, a novel about the Kent State shootings, and *Fade*, a novel of Bratislava. He has written numerous articles and reviews on literature, art, and film, and is also the author of the Quarry Books series: ten booklets about Vermonters in the American grain. He divides his time between Vermont and Bratislava.

SELECTED DALKEY ARCHIVE TITLES

MICHAL AJVAZ, *The Golden Age.*
The Other City.
PIERRE ALBERT-BIROT, *Grabinoulor.*
YUZ ALESHKOVSKY, *Kangaroo.*
FELIPE ALFAU, *Chromos.*
Locos.
IVAN ÂNGELO, *The Celebration.*
The Tower of Glass.
ANTÓNIO LOBO ANTUNES, *Knowledge of Hell.*
The Splendor of Portugal.
ALAIN ARIAS-MISSON, *Theatre of Incest.*
JOHN ASHBERY AND JAMES SCHUYLER,
A Nest of Ninnies.
ROBERT ASHLEY, *Perfect Lives.*
GABRIELA AVIGUR-ROTEM, *Heatwave and Crazy Birds.*
DJUNA BARNES, *Ladies Almanack.*
Ryder.
JOHN BARTH, *LETTERS.*
Sabbatical.
DONALD BARTHELME, *The King.*
Paradise.
SVETISLAV BASARA, *Chinese Letter.*
MIQUEL BAUÇÀ, *The Siege in the Room.*
RENÉ BELLETTO, *Dying.*
MAREK BIEŃCZYK, *Transparency.*
ANDREI BITOV, *Pushkin House.*
ANDREJ BLATNIK, *You Do Understand.*
LOUIS PAUL BOON, *Chapel Road.*
My Little War.
Summer in Termuren.
ROGER BOYLAN, *Killoyle.*
IGNÁCIO DE LOYOLA BRANDÃO,
Anonymous Celebrity.
Zero.
BONNIE BREMSER, *Troia: Mexican Memoirs.*
CHRISTINE BROOKE-ROSE, *Amalgamemnon.*
BRIGID BROPHY, *In Transit.*
GERALD L. BRUNS, *Modern Poetry and the Idea of Language.*
GABRIELLE BURTON, *Heartbreak Hotel.*
MICHEL BUTOR, *Degrees.*
Mobile.
G. CABRERA INFANTE, *Infante's Inferno.*
Three Trapped Tigers.
JULIETA CAMPOS,
The Fear of Losing Eurydice.
ANNE CARSON, *Eros the Bittersweet.*
ORLY CASTEL-BLOOM, *Dolly City.*
LOUIS-FERDINAND CÉLINE, *Castle to Castle.*
Conversations with Professor Y.
London Bridge.
Normance.
North.
Rigadoon.
MARIE CHAIX, *The Laurels of Lake Constance.*
HUGO CHARTERIS, *The Tide Is Right.*
ERIC CHEVILLARD, *Demolishing Nisard.*
MARC CHOLODENKO, *Mordechai Schamz.*
JOSHUA COHEN, *Witz.*
EMILY HOLMES COLEMAN, *The Shutter of Snow.*
ROBERT COOVER, *A Night at the Movies.*
STANLEY CRAWFORD, *Log of the S.S. The Mrs Unguentine.*
Some Instructions to My Wife.
RENÉ CREVEL, *Putting My Foot in It.*
RALPH CUSACK, *Cadenza.*
NICHOLAS DELBANCO, *The Count of Concord.*
Sherbrookes.
NIGEL DENNIS, *Cards of Identity.*
PETER DIMOCK, *A Short Rhetoric for Leaving the Family.*
ARIEL DORFMAN, *Konfidenz.*
COLEMAN DOWELL,
Island People.
Too Much Flesh and Jabez.
ARKADII DRAGOMOSHCHENKO, *Dust.*
RIKKI DUCORNET, *The Complete Butcher's Tales.*
The Fountains of Neptune.
The Jade Cabinet.
Phosphor in Dreamland.
WILLIAM EASTLAKE, *The Bamboo Bed.*
Castle Keep.
Lyric of the Circle Heart.
JEAN ECHENOZ, *Chopin's Move.*
STANLEY ELKIN, *A Bad Man.*
Criers and Kibitzers, Kibitzers and Criers.
The Dick Gibson Show.
The Franchiser.
The Living End.
Mrs. Ted Bliss.
FRANÇOIS EMMANUEL, *Invitation to a Voyage.*
SALVADOR ESPRIU, *Ariadne in the Grotesque Labyrinth.*
LESLIE A. FIEDLER, *Love and Death in the American Novel.*
JUAN FILLOY, *Op Oloop.*
ANDY FITCH, *Pop Poetics.*
GUSTAVE FLAUBERT, *Bouvard and Pécuchet.*
KASS FLEISHER, *Talking out of School.*
FORD MADOX FORD,
The March of Literature.
JON FOSSE, *Aliss at the Fire.*
Melancholy.
MAX FRISCH, *I'm Not Stiller.*
Man in the Holocene.
CARLOS FUENTES, *Christopher Unborn.*
Distant Relations.
Terra Nostra.
Where the Air Is Clear.
TAKEHIKO FUKUNAGA, *Flowers of Grass.*
WILLIAM GADDIS, *J R.*
The Recognitions.
JANICE GALLOWAY, *Foreign Parts.*
The Trick Is to Keep Breathing.
WILLIAM H. GASS, *Cartesian Sonata and Other Novellas.*
Finding a Form.
A Temple of Texts.
The Tunnel.
Willie Masters' Lonesome Wife.
GÉRARD GAVARRY, *Hoppla! 1 2 3.*
ETIENNE GILSON,
The Arts of the Beautiful.
Forms and Substances in the Arts.
C. S. GISCOMBE, *Giscome Road.*
Here.
DOUGLAS GLOVER, *Bad News of the Heart.*
WITOLD GOMBROWICZ,
A Kind of Testament.
PAULO EMÍLIO SALES GOMES, *P's Three Women.*
GEORGI GOSPODINOV, *Natural Novel.*
JUAN GOYTISOLO, *Count Julian.*
Juan the Landless.
Makbara.
Marks of Identity.

FOR A FULL LIST OF PUBLICATIONS, VISIT:
www.dalkeyarchive.com

SELECTED DALKEY ARCHIVE TITLES

Henry Green, *Back.*
Blindness.
Concluding.
Doting.
Nothing.
Jack Green, *Fire the Bastards!*
Jiří Gruša, *The Questionnaire.*
Mela Hartwig, *Am I a Redundant Human Being?*
John Hawkes, *The Passion Artist.*
Whistlejacket.
Elizabeth Heighway, ed., *Contemporary Georgian Fiction.*
Aleksandar Hemon, ed., *Best European Fiction.*
Aidan Higgins, *Balcony of Europe.*
Blind Man's Bluff
Bornholm Night-Ferry.
Flotsam and Jetsam.
Langrishe, Go Down.
Scenes from a Receding Past.
Keizo Hino, *Isle of Dreams.*
Kazushi Hosaka, *Plainsong.*
Aldous Huxley, *Antic Hay.*
Crome Yellow.
Point Counter Point.
Those Barren Leaves.
Time Must Have a Stop.
Naoyuki Ii, *The Shadow of a Blue Cat.*
Gert Jonke, *The Distant Sound.*
Geometric Regional Novel.
Homage to Czerny.
The System of Vienna.
Jacques Jouet, *Mountain R.*
Savage.
Upstaged.
Mieko Kanai, *The Word Book.*
Yoram Kaniuk, *Life on Sandpaper.*
Hugh Kenner, *Flaubert.*
Joyce and Beckett: The Stoic Comedians.
Joyce's Voices.
Danilo Kiš, *The Attic.*
Garden, Ashes.
The Lute and the Scars
Psalm 44.
A Tomb for Boris Davidovich.
Anita Konkka, *A Fool's Paradise.*
George Konrád, *The City Builder.*
Tadeusz Konwicki, *A Minor Apocalypse.*
The Polish Complex.
Menis Koumandareas, *Koula.*
Elaine Kraf, *The Princess of 72nd Street.*
Jim Krusoe, *Iceland.*
Ayşe Kulin, *Farewell: A Mansion in Occupied Istanbul.*
Emilio Lascano Tegui, *On Elegance While Sleeping.*
Eric Laurrent, *Do Not Touch.*
Violette Leduc, *La Bâtarde.*
Edouard Levé, *Autoportrait.*
Suicide.
Mario Levi, *Istanbul Was a Fairy Tale.*
Deborah Levy, *Billy and Girl.*
José Lezama Lima, *Paradiso.*
Rosa Liksom, *Dark Paradise.*
Osman Lins, *Avalovara.*
The Queen of the Prisons of Greece.
Alf Mac Lochlainn, *The Corpus in the Library.*
Out of Focus.
Ron Loewinsohn, *Magnetic Field(s).*
Mina Loy, *Stories and Essays of Mina Loy.*
D. Keith Mano, *Take Five.*
Micheline Aharonian Marcom, *The Mirror in the Well.*
Ben Marcus, *The Age of Wire and String.*
Wallace Markfield, *Teitlebaum's Window.*
To an Early Grave.
David Markson, *Reader's Block.*
Wittgenstein's Mistress.
Carole Maso, *AVA.*
Ladislav Matejka and Krystyna Pomorska, eds., *Readings in Russian Poetics: Formalist and Structuralist Views.*
Harry Mathews, *Cigarettes.*
The Conversions.
The Human Country: New and Collected Stories.
The Journalist.
My Life in CIA.
Singular Pleasures.
The Sinking of the Odradek Stadium.
Tlooth.
Joseph McElroy, *Night Soul and Other Stories.*
Abdelwahab Meddeb, *Talismano.*
Gerhard Meier, *Isle of the Dead.*
Herman Melville, *The Confidence-Man.*
Amanda Michalopoulou, *I'd Like.*
Steven Millhauser, *The Barnum Museum.*
In the Penny Arcade.
Ralph J. Mills, Jr., *Essays on Poetry.*
Momus, *The Book of Jokes.*
Christine Montalbetti, *The Origin of Man.*
Western.
Olive Moore, *Spleen.*
Nicholas Mosley, *Accident.*
Assassins.
Catastrophe Practice.
Experience and Religion.
A Garden of Trees.
Hopeful Monsters.
Imago Bird.
Impossible Object.
Inventing God.
Judith.
Look at the Dark.
Natalie Natalia.
Serpent.
Time at War.
Warren Motte, *Fables of the Novel: French Fiction since 1990.*
Fiction Now: The French Novel in the 21st Century.
Oulipo: A Primer of Potential Literature.
Gerald Murnane, *Barley Patch.*
Inland.
Yves Navarre, *Our Share of Time.*
Sweet Tooth.
Dorothy Nelson, *In Night's City.*
Tar and Feathers.
Eshkol Nevo, *Homesick.*
Wilfrido D. Nolledo, *But for the Lovers.*
Flann O'Brien, *At Swim-Two-Birds.*
The Best of Myles.
The Dalkey Archive.
The Hard Life.
The Poor Mouth.

SELECTED DALKEY ARCHIVE TITLES

The Third Policeman.
Claude Ollier, *The Mise-en-Scène.*
Wert and the Life Without End.
Giovanni Orelli, *Walaschek's Dream.*
Patrik Ouředník, *Europeana.*
The Opportune Moment, 1855.
Boris Pahor, *Necropolis.*
Fernando del Paso, *News from the Empire.*
Palinuro of Mexico.
Robert Pinget, *The Inquisitory.*
Mahu or The Material.
Trio.
Manuel Puig, *Betrayed by Rita Hayworth.*
The Buenos Aires Affair.
Heartbreak Tango.
Raymond Queneau, *The Last Days.*
Odile.
Pierrot Mon Ami.
Saint Glinglin.
Ann Quin, *Berg.*
Passages.
Three.
Tripticks.
Ishmael Reed, *The Free-Lance Pallbearers.*
The Last Days of Louisiana Red.
Ishmael Reed: The Plays.
Juice!
Reckless Eyeballing.
The Terrible Threes.
The Terrible Twos.
Yellow Back Radio Broke-Down.
Jasia Reichardt, *15 Journeys Warsaw to London.*
Noëlle Revaz, *With the Animals.*
João Ubaldo Ribeiro, *House of the Fortunate Buddhas.*
Jean Ricardou, *Place Names.*
Rainer Maria Rilke, *The Notebooks of Malte Laurids Brigge.*
Julián Ríos, *The House of Ulysses.*
Larva: A Midsummer Night's Babel.
Poundemonium.
Procession of Shadows.
Augusto Roa Bastos, *I the Supreme.*
Daniël Robberechts, *Arriving in Avignon.*
Jean Rolin, *The Explosion of the Radiator Hose.*
Olivier Rolin, *Hotel Crystal.*
Alix Cleo Roubaud, *Alix's Journal.*
Jacques Roubaud, *The Form of a City Changes Faster, Alas, Than the Human Heart.*
The Great Fire of London.
Hortense in Exile.
Hortense Is Abducted.
The Loop.
Mathematics:
The Plurality of Worlds of Lewis.
The Princess Hoppy.
Some Thing Black.
Raymond Roussel, *Impressions of Africa.*
Vedrana Rudan, *Night.*
Stig Sæterbakken, *Siamese.*
Self Control.
Lydie Salvayre, *The Company of Ghosts.*
The Lecture.
The Power of Flies.
Luis Rafael Sánchez, *Macho Camacho's Beat.*
Severo Sarduy, *Cobra & Maitreya.*
Nathalie Sarraute, *Do You Hear Them?*
Martereau.
The Planetarium.
Arno Schmidt, *Collected Novellas.*
Collected Stories.
Nobodaddy's Children.
Two Novels.
Asaf Schurr, *Motti.*
Gail Scott, *My Paris.*
Damion Searls, *What We Were Doing and Where We Were Going.*
June Akers Seese, *Is This What Other Women Feel Too?*
What Waiting Really Means.
Bernard Share, *Inish.*
Transit.
Viktor Shklovsky, *Bowstring.*
Knight's Move.
A Sentimental Journey: Memoirs 1917–1922.
Energy of Delusion: A Book on Plot.
Literature and Cinematography.
Theory of Prose.
Third Factory.
Zoo, or Letters Not about Love.
Pierre Siniac, *The Collaborators.*
Kjersti A. Skomsvold, *The Faster I Walk, the Smaller I Am.*
Josef Škvorecký, *The Engineer of Human Souls.*
Gilbert Sorrentino, *Aberration of Starlight.*
Blue Pastoral.
Crystal Vision.
Imaginative Qualities of Actual Things.
Mulligan Stew.
Pack of Lies.
Red the Fiend.
The Sky Changes.
Something Said.
Splendide-Hôtel.
Steelwork.
Under the Shadow.
W. M. Spackman, *The Complete Fiction.*
Andrzej Stasiuk, *Dukla.*
Fado.
Gertrude Stein, *The Making of Americans.*
A Novel of Thank You.
Lars Svendsen, *A Philosophy of Evil.*
Piotr Szewc, *Annihilation.*
Gonçalo M. Tavares, *Jerusalem.*
Joseph Walser's Machine.
Learning to Pray in the Age of Technique.
Lucian Dan Teodorovici, *Our Circus Presents . . .*
Nikanor Teratologen, *Assisted Living.*
Stefan Themerson, *Hobson's Island.*
The Mystery of the Sardine.
Tom Harris.
Taeko Tomioka, *Building Waves.*
John Toomey, *Sleepwalker.*
Jean-Philippe Toussaint, *The Bathroom.*
Camera.
Monsieur.
Reticence.
Running Away.
Self-Portrait Abroad.
Television.
The Truth about Marie.

FOR A FULL LIST OF PUBLICATIONS, VISIT:
www.dalkeyarchive.com

Dumitru Tsepeneag, *Hotel Europa.*
The Necessary Marriage.
Pigeon Post.
Vain Art of the Fugue.
Esther Tusquets, *Stranded.*
Dubravka Ugresic, *Lend Me Your Character.*
Thank You for Not Reading.
Tor Ulven, *Replacement.*
Mati Unt, *Brecht at Night.*
Diary of a Blood Donor.
Things in the Night.
Álvaro Uribe and Olivia Sears, eds., *Best of Contemporary Mexican Fiction.*
Eloy Urroz, *Friction.*
The Obstacles.
Luisa Valenzuela, *Dark Desires and the Others.*
He Who Searches.
Paul Verhaeghen, *Omega Minor.*
Aglaja Veteranyi, *Why the Child Is Cooking in the Polenta.*
Boris Vian, *Heartsnatcher.*
Llorenç Villalonga, *The Dolls' Room.*
Toomas Vint, *An Unending Landscape.*
Ornela Vorpsi, *The Country Where No One Ever Dies.*
Austryn Wainhouse, *Hedyphagetica.*
Curtis White, *America's Magic Mountain.*
The Idea of Home.
Memories of My Father Watching TV.
Requiem.
Diane Williams, *Excitability: Selected Stories.*
Romancer Erector.
Douglas Woolf, *Wall to Wall.*
Ya! & John-Juan.
Jay Wright, *Polynomials and Pollen.*
The Presentable Art of Reading Absence.
Philip Wylie, *Generation of Vipers.*
Marguerite Young, *Angel in the Forest.*
Miss MacIntosh, My Darling.
Reyoung, *Unbabbling.*
Vlado Žabot, *The Succubus.*
Zoran Živković, *Hidden Camera.*
Louis Zukofsky, *Collected Fiction.*
Vitomil Zupan, *Minuet for Guitar.*
Scott Zwiren, *God Head.*

www.ingramcontent.com/pod-product-compliance
Lightning Source LLC
Jackson TN
JSHW021917190426
101040JS00042B/343

* 9 7 8 1 5 6 4 7 8 8 8 7 0 *